Growing Forward Together

A Socio- Emotional and Wellness Workbook

A K-12 Activity Guide for
Nurturing Socio-Emotional
Wellness and Character Growth

written by
Tamara Pray Frazier
with Tamara Bogan, LPC

Copyright © 2025 by Tamara Pray Frazier & Tamara Bogan, LPC

Growing Forward Together: A K-12 Activity Guide for Nurturing Socio-Emotional Wellness and Character Growth

All rights reserved. No part of this publication may be reproduced, distributed, or transmitted in any form or by any means, including photocopying, recording, or other electronic or mechanical methods, without the prior written permission of the publisher, except in the case of brief quotations embodied in critical reviews and certain other noncommercial uses permitted by copyright law.

Interior design by Toni R. Settles

The main character, Daisy, and other characters from the Walking With Grace Series were illustrated by J'Aaron Merchant.

Printed in the United States
First Edition: August 2025
ISBN: 978-1-7361667-7-2

Publishing Services provided by
Julian's Legacy Publishers

Table of Contents

Introduction 1

Dear Trusted Adults 2

The Importance of Character Development 3

Vocabulary Definitions 4

Character Traits Crossword Puzzle 6

Dear Trusted Adult 9

Esteem Building Activities 10
    Affirmation Ball 10
    Short-Term Goals 11
    Affirmation Jar 13
    I am Possible 15
    Positive Pieces of Me 16
    Journal Writing Prompts 17
    Mirror Me Journal Writing & Sharing 19

Seed Lessons 22

Dear Bus Drivers 25

Vocabulary Fill in the Blank 26

Affirmation Mirror Activity 28

Superpower Shield Activity 29

Lesson Plans 31

Dear Guardian 35

Developing Self-Esteem & Self-Worth 36

Discussing Questions 40

Walk in My Shoes: Empathy and Individuality Circle 47

Dear Grandparent 50

Soft Skills 51

Mindfulness 53

Closing Words 56

"It is easier to build strong children than to fix broken men."

Frederick Douglass

Introduction

Welcome to a journey of confidence, kindness, and character development!

This book was created to help you see how amazing, unique, and powerful you truly are. Inside, you'll find inspiring stories, fun activities, and thoughtful questions that will guide you in celebrating who you are—inside and out.

As you read, you'll explore important ideas like self-esteem, diversity, empathy, and friendship. You'll also discover simple mindfulness practices to help you feel calm, focused, and ready to shine in any situation.

Remember: there's no one else in the world exactly like you. Your thoughts, talents, and personality make you your own kind of beautiful.

Let's dive in and explore what makes you....**you!**

In addition, this book includes appreciation letters to those who matter.

Thank you for all that you do.

Enjoy and Grow Forward!

Dear Trusted Adult,

Tamara & Tamara here!! Before getting started, we just want to take a moment to encourage you as an educator, parent, counselor, friend, auntie, uncle, or trusted advisor. Whether you wear one of these hats, or a combination of several, YOU ARE the key that will unlock the potential, hopes, imagination and possibilities of our future generations. And as such, you need and deserve to be uplifted and encouraged as you change the world!! I know our job is heavy... but what hope do our children have if WE don't pour into them and lay a solid foundation for them to grow forward? What hope do we have as an older generation if our youth don't have the tools to continue to grow, and evolve in this ever-changing world? And how do we equip them with the tools needed?

Well, I am glad you asked.

We must **INTENTIONALLY** instill values into our children to positively develop their character as early as possible. If we want them to behave in a certain manner, then we must not only tell them, but **SHOW THEM.** Model the behavior you want to see, then grasp each teachable moment as they come to reinforce your expectations. Remember, words hold power, especially in the moment, but experiences sustain over time. If we don't teach them, who will?

- If we teach them **HONESTY**, they will honor their commitments.
- If we teach them **CONFIDENCE**, they learn how capable they are!
- If we teach them **SELF-LOVE**, they learn to not sacrifice themselves.
- If we teach them how to **ADAPT**, they learn how to advance the world.
- If we teach them **RESPECT**, they learn to be receptive to our differences.
- If we teach them how to **COPE**, they learn how to stand strong in the face of adversity.
- If we teach them **ACCOUNTABILITY**, they learn to take ownership of their actions.
- If we teach them to **COMMUNICATE**, they learn to express their needs and concerns.

WITHOUT HESITATION...

We are the key.
Thank you for making the decision to Grow Forward with us!

Tamara & Tamara

The Importance of Character Development

Your Own Kind of Beautiful

Fostering character development is crucial in shaping children into positive, productive adults. Character education serves as the foundation for raising children who not only survive but also thrive in our interconnected world.

Character Development · Vocabulary

Citizenship
Compassion
Responsibility
Confidence
Courage
Empathy
Grace
Gratitude
Honesty
Kindness
Self-Esteem
Self-Respect
Self-Worth
Accountability
Communication
Respect
Adapt

Vocabulary Definitions

Before You Begin

Throughout this book, you'll come across certain words that are important to understand. These words will help you get the most out of each activity and story. Use the definitions below as a guide, and feel free to revisit them anytime you need a reminder.

Citizenship — Showing good character, respecting others, and their property and treating others as you would like to be treated.

Compassion — Showing kindness, caring and a willingness to help others.

Responsibility — Doing what you're supposed to do and being trusted to do the right thing.

Confidence — Feeling sure of yourself or trusting in someone or something.

Courage — Choosing to do the right thing even when you are afraid.

Empathy — The ability to feel and understand what someone else is going through.

Grace — Receiving things you do not deserve, simply because you are loved.

Gratitude — Being thankful for the things you have.

Honesty — Being truthful in the things you say and do.

Kindness — Being caring, selfless, helpful and gentle.

Self-Esteem — How we feel about ourselves.

Vocabulary Definitions

Accountability — The practice of being held responsible.

Communication — Sending and receiving information. Talking and body language are examples.

Respect — A feeling of deep admiration for someone or something.

Adapt — Adjusting to new surroundings or conditions.

Self-Respect — Feeling good about who you are and the choices you make.

Self-Worth — Liking yourself and believing you are worthy and belong.

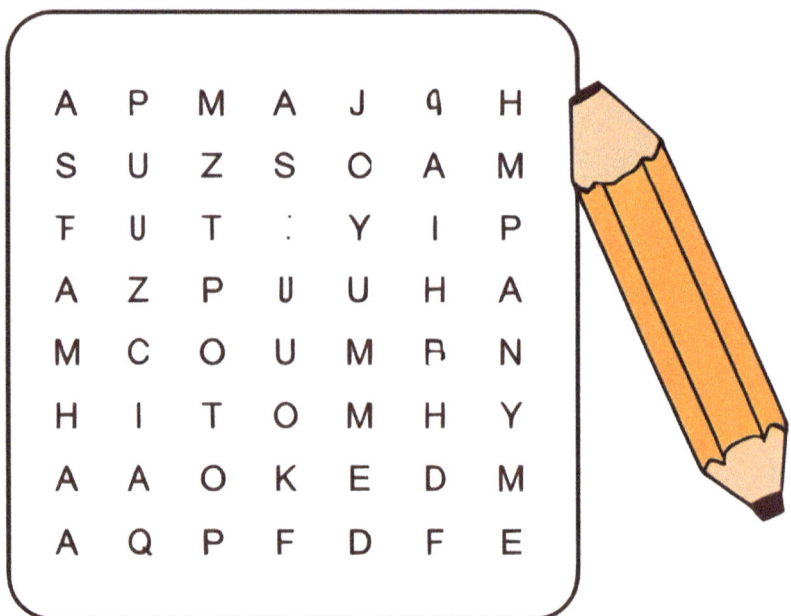

Character Traits Word Search Puzzle

Are you ready to go on a word hunt?

Each word in this puzzle is a powerful trait that helps you become your best self at school, at home, and in your community. Words like kindness, honesty, and courage are hidden across the puzzle. Look carefully, they might be going left to right, right to left, up, down, or even diagonally!

Here's how to play:
Use the Word Bank to guide your search.
Circle or highlight each word as you find it in the puzzle.

When you find a word, think about how YOU can show that trait in real life!

Try to find all 17 words on the next page. When you are done, pick your favorite word and write a sentence or draw a picture to show what it means to you.

Do your best to find the vocabulary words in the crossword puzzle.

a	c	c	o	u	n	t	a	b	i	l	i	t	y	r
s	c	o	m	m	u	n	i	i	a	t	i	o	n	e
e	s	s	c	i	t	i	z	e	n	s	h	i	p	s
l	e	e	g	o	t	r	e	s	t	c	z	o	g	p
f	l	l	r	h	m	i	r	e	s	p	e	c	t	o
r	f	f	a	u	a	p	r	n	y	e	e	n	a	n
e	e	w	t	k	c	m	a	w	g	r	a	c	e	s
s	s	o	i	i	o	u	l	s	t	i	o	n	e	i
p	t	r	t	a	u	l	o	w	s	n	g	a	e	b
e	e	t	u	p	r	s	s	i	o	i	p	a	c	i
c	e	h	d	r	a	r	i	t	e	r	o	b	i	l
t	m	n	e	s	g	y	a	d	a	p	t	n	o	i
s	p	s	h	j	e	c	o	n	f	i	d	e	n	t
h	o	n	e	s	t	y	i	e	m	p	a	t	h	y
t	l	m	k	a	k	i	n	d	n	e	s	s	e	q

Citizenship   Empathy   Kindness   Accountability

Compassion   Grace   Self esteem   Communication

Responsibility   Gratitude   Self respect   Respect

Confident   Honesty   Self worth   Adapt

Courage

See answers on page 57.

Use your favorite vocabulary word to describe yourself.

Dear Trusted Adult,

Everyday is a new beginning. Today, take some time to appreciate your kindness and understanding attitude as you face challenging moments with your children. Even though it doesn't feel like it, you are making a positive impact! Keep going. We believe in you!

With love,
T & T

Esteem Building Activities

Affirmation Ball Game

Objective:
To build self-esteem and encourage positive self-expression by having children share affirming statements about themselves.

Participants:
Minimum of 3 children (ideal for small or large group settings)

Materials Needed:
A medium-sized ball (such as a beach ball) with fill-in-the-blank affirmations or positive prompts written on it using a permanent marker.

Sample prompts:
The thing I love about my hair is _____.
My favorite thing about me is _____, because _____.
I AM _____.
I feel happy when _____.
I feel good when _____.
My happy place is_____.
I feel amazing when _____.
My favorite article of clothing is _____, because it makes me feel _____.
When I need a pick me up, I _____.
_____ makes me smile.

Instructions:
Have the group form a circle or stand in an open area.
One child starts by gently tossing the ball to someone else in the group.
The child who catches the ball will read the prompt closest to their right thumb and complete the sentence out loud.
After sharing their affirmation, they toss the ball to another person.
Continue the game until everyone has had multiple turns.

Tips for Success:
Encourage students to speak clearly and with confidence.
Adults or group leaders can model responses to set the tone.
Remind participants that all answers should be kind and supportive.

Short-Term Goal Activity

Objective:
To help children practice goal setting and build awareness around personal growth.

Participants:
Minimum of 2 people (can be done in pairs, small groups, or as a class activity)

Materials Needed:
Soft dice
Paper or a journal
Pens, pencils, or other writing utensils

Instructions:
Each child will take a turn rolling the soft dice.
The number that lands face up represents how many short-term goals the child must create and share out loud. After sharing, the child will write their goals in a journal or on paper to keep track of their progress.

Encourage children to think about goals that are age-appropriate, specific, and achievable like improving a skill, helping at home, or reading a new book.

Revisit these goals regularly to reflect on progress and celebrate growth.

Note:
This activity encourages communication, self-reflection, and motivation, and works well in both classroom and home settings.

Affirmation Jar Activity

Objective:
To help children develop positive self-talk and boost their self-esteem through daily affirmations.

Materials Needed:
A mason jar (or any type of container)
Small, colorful sticky notes or cut pieces of paper
Pen or marker, or other writing utensils

Instructions:
Have each child write a positive affirmation on a sticky note or small slip of paper. Fold the notes and place them inside the jar. Each morning, the child will pull one affirmation from the jar and read it out loud multiple times with confidence and enthusiasm. Encourage the child to say the affirmation in front of a mirror if possible.

An adult (parent, caregiver, or teacher) should be present to reinforce the affirmation and offer encouragement.

Setting:
This activity is ideal for both classroom and home environments. Consistency and adult involvement help children absorb the positive messages more deeply.

Note:
Sample affirmations are provided on the next page for inspiration.

Affirmations Page

1. Today I choose happiness.
2. I am beautiful inside and out.
3. Today I will share my smile with the world.
4. I am kind to others.
5. I can change the world.
6. I am smart.
7. My voice is important.
8. Today is a perfect day to make a difference.
9. I will encourage someone who is struggling.
10. I am considerate of others.
11. I can succeed even when things are hard.
12. I am doing fine!
13. I am loved.
14. My family is perfect for me.
15. I am important.
16. There is only one of me. I am unique.
17. I deserve to be treated with love and kindness.
18. I think positive thoughts.
19. Great things are happening in my life.
20. All of my dreams are aligning.
21. I radiate positive energy and thoughts.
22. My words are motivating and healing.
23. I am going to have the best day ever!
24. I make good choices.
25. I am proud of myself.
26. I am courageous.
27. I won't give up.
28. I will not give up.
29. I am excited to learn something new.
30. Today I will try something new!

I Am Possible Activity

Objective:
To help children build self-esteem by encouraging them to think positively about themselves and celebrate their unique qualities.

Materials Needed:
Drawing paper or construction paper
Colorful markers, colored pencils, or any writing/drawing utensils

Instructions:
Have each child write "I AM" in large, bold letters in the center of their paper. Around the "I AM" statement, students will write words that describe who they are such as kind, creative, brave, funny, or helpful—using different colors.

Encourage them to be creative with their word choices and to express their individuality. Children may also decorate their page to reflect their personality, turning it into a colorful self-portrait of words.

Once completed, invite students to share their Word Portraits with each other to build community and confidence.

Setting:
This activity can be done in a classroom, group setting, or one-on-one at home. Sharing aloud fosters positive group dynamics and self-expression.

Positive Pieces of Me Activity

Items Needed:

Magazines or newspapers

Markers

Poster board or construction paper (depending on the size you want them to do).

Activity:

Have each student create a collage of pictures that describe them. They can use a combination of photos and words to complete their collage.

Journal Writing Prompts

(Encourage students to write at least three sentences. Assign more if you like.)

I am proud of myself because I did…
I am at my happiest when I am…
The one thing I wish I could change about myself for positive growth is…
The most important thing in the world to me is…
The thing I am most proud of is…
When I am at home, I love to…
If I am feeling sad, I usually…
My best friend is… We have the most fun when we…
My happy place is…
I am most grateful for…
Reflect on your family. What do you like most about being a member of your family?
Reflect on a mistake you made. How did you feel and what did you do to correct it?
Reflect on a time you became angry. What made you angry and what did you do about it?
The happiest day ever was when…
Describe a time when you were really happy. What made you smile so big?

Write three sentences that you feel best describes you.

Mirror Me: Journal Writing & Sharing Activity:

Objective:
To build self-awareness, confidence, and connection through writing and peer encouragement.

Instructions:

Choose a Prompt:
Each student selects one journal prompt from the list to write about. Encourage them to write at least three sentences and include why their response is important to them.

Creative Expression:
After writing, students will draw a small illustration that matches what they wrote (e.g., if their happy place is the beach, they draw it).

Partner Share – "Mirror Me":
Pair students up. Each student takes turns reading their journal entry to their partner.

The partner must:
Listen carefully
Respond with a compliment or positive reflection starting with:
"I see you because…" or "I think it's awesome that you…"

Group Reflection (Optional):
Choose a few students to share their writing and artwork with the class.
As a class, reflect on how everyone has different strengths and happy places, and how that's what makes the class special.

Materials Needed:
Activity book or lined paper
Colored pencils/crayons
Prompt list displayed or printed

Mirror Me – Journal Writing Prompts

When I look in the mirror, I see someone who is…

One thing I love about my personality is…

Something I'm really good at is…

I feel most confident when I…

One challenge I've overcome is…

I feel happy when…

If I could give myself one kind message every morning, it would be…

My friends would describe me as…

One way I show kindness to others is…

Something that makes me unique is…

I am proud of myself because…

My favorite thing about my appearance is…

One goal I have for myself this month is…

I feel strong when I…

I am fearfully & wonderfully made because…

Select one journal prompt from the list to write about.

Seed Lesson

Title:

Writing a Children's Book: Creating Engaging Characters, Developing a Compelling Plot, and Using Age-Appropriate Language & Themes

Instructional Model:

5E Model – Engage, Explore, Explain, Elaborate, Evaluate

Lesson Duration:

45–52 minutes

Objective:

Students will demonstrate proficiency in writing a children's book by creating engaging characters, developing a compelling plot, and using age-appropriate language and themes.

Key Vocabulary:

Plot   **Children's book**   **Engaging**

Characters   **Themes**   **Compelling**

Age-appropriate language

Seed Lesson Outline

Engage (5 minutes)

Display a variety of children's books.

- Ask students to share their favorite childhood book and what made it engaging.
- Discuss why strong characters, compelling plots, and age-appropriate language/themes are important.
- Introduce the lesson objective and explain that students will create their own children's book.

2. Explore (10 minutes)

Provide children's books from different genres for students to review.

In pairs or small groups, students analyze characters, plot development, and language.

Discuss findings as a class and compile a list of characteristics that make children's books successful.

3. Explain (10 minutes)

Teach how to create relatable, interesting, and memorable characters.

Discuss story structures and plot elements: conflict, resolution, climax.

Explain how age-appropriate language and themes enhance understanding and enjoyment for the target audience.

4. Elaborate (15 minutes)

In pairs or groups, students brainstorm ideas for their own book, focusing on characters, plot, and language.

Use guiding questions and prompts to encourage creativity.

Circulate to offer feedback, answer questions, and provide support.

5. Evaluate (10–12 minutes)

Students share a brief summary of their book idea with the class.

Encourage constructive feedback and questions from peers.

Students reflect on what they learned about characters, plot, and language/themes.

Closure:

Review the importance of engaging characters, compelling plots, and age-appropriate language/themes.

Connect back to students' favorite childhood books from the opening activity. Highlight how applying these elements can strengthen their own writing.

Differentiation Options:

Offer extra guidance for students who need help generating ideas or understanding age-appropriate content. Challenge advanced students to explore complex plot structures or experiment with narrative techniques. Provide resources such as visuals, graphic organizers, or sentence starters to support different learning styles.

Assessment:

Monitor participation and engagement throughout.

Check students' ability to identify and apply key elements during the Explore phase. Evaluate creativity, critical thinking, and mastery through their book ideas and reflections.

Optionally, assign a written reflection or short children's story as a summative assessment.

Dear Bus Driver,

You are tasked with making sure your precious passengers make it safely to and from school. Your occupation may feel thankless at times, but you are a vital asset to families. You get up early on chilly mornings and make sure the bus is warm before students board your bus. You greet them with a kind smile which helps set the tone for their day. You also communicate with parents and school officials concerning the students that you transport.

You do all of that and more effectively while navigating new routes, driver shortages, inclement weather conditions and the excited voices on your bus. Never underestimate your calling, you are and will always be an essential employee in education.

With love,
T & T

Fill In the Blank: Vocabulary

Compassion   Confident   Empathy   Self-Respect   Self-Esteem

Kindness   Citizenship   Grace   Honesty

Courage   Communication   Adapt   Accountability

Responsibility   Gratitude   Self-Worth   Respect

1. It takes _____ to stand up for others, but I do so every day.

2. We should be kind and show _____ to others every day.

3. I wake up with _____ in my heart. I am thankful for my life.

4. I feel good about myself and the choices I make for myself. I have _____.

5. My friend is sad. I have _____ for her.

6. I am willing to help others in need. I show _____ in words and deeds.

7. I show good _____ in school. I follow all the rules.

8. It is my _____ to make up my bed everyday.

9. I am _____ that I know all my site words.

10. My teacher showed _____ when she gave me more time to complete my assignment.

11. We should _____ our elders and each other.

12. _____ is one way to show people you are trustworthy.

13. Moving to a new school means we must _____ to a different environment.

14. Good _____ is an important part of relationships.

15. My _____ determines how much I love and respect myself.

Affirmation Mirror Activity

Objective:

Encourage kids to speak kindly to themselves using a hand-held mirror.

Materials:

Handheld or traditional wall mirror.

Instructions:

Give each child a mirror or have them stand in front of a mirror.

Then prompt them to say kind things to themselves in the mirror.

Affirmation Mirror Prompts

(If a mirror is unavailable students can read them aloud in unison or individually.)

I am smart and capable of learning new things.
I am kind to myself and others.
I am brave enough to try, even when it's hard.
I am unique, and that makes me special.
I am worthy of love and respect.
I am creative and full of good ideas.
I am proud of who I am becoming.
I am a good friend who listens and cares.
I am enough, just as I am.
I am confident in my voice and my choices.
I am strong inside and out.
I am grateful for who I am today.
I am beautiful, inside and out.
I am important, and my thoughts matter.
I am a helper who makes the world better.
I am learning and growing every single day.
I am full of amazing ideas that can help others.
I am special because there is only one me.
I am able to handle whatever comes my way.
I am a problem-solver who doesn't give up.
I am someone who makes others smile.
I am loved by people who care about me.
I am a leader who can inspire others.
I am worthy of reaching my dreams.
I am happy being me.

My Superpower Shield

Objective:
Help kids identify their strengths and values.

Materials:
Printable shield template, colored pencils, stickers.

Instructions:
Give each child a blank shield divided into four sections. (Blank shield provided on the next page.)

Label sections:
I am good at
I've overcome
One day I will
I dream of

Kids decorate the shield with drawings or words that match each prompt.

Share with the group or keep as a personal reminder of inner strength.

Your Superpower Shield

Color and decorate the shield with drawings or words that match each prompt.

I'm good at	I've overcome
One day I will	**I dream of**

Lesson Plans

Building Self-Esteem through Your Kind of Beautiful

Grade Level:
Middle School
(Students Grade 6-8)

Unit Topic:
Applying social-emotional learning strategies to develop and enhance personal self-esteem and self-worth.

Book:
Your Own Kind of Beautiful

Instructional Model:
5E Model (Engage, Explore, Explain, Elaborate, Evaluate)

Duration:
45-52 minutes

Objective:
Students will demonstrate the ability to apply a range of social-emotional learning strategies to develop and enhance their personal self-esteem and self-worth through the utilization of the children's book, "Your Own Kind of Beautiful"

Key Vocabulary:
Self-esteem
Self-worth
Positive self-talk
Growth mindset
Empathy
Resilience
Gratitude
Mindfulness

Materials:
"Your Own Kind of Beautiful" by Tamara Pray Frazier (one copy per student or pair)
Chart paper and markers
Sticky notes
Index cards
Writing materials (pencils, pens, or colored pencils)

Procedure:

Engage (5 minutes):
1. Begin the lesson by displaying the cover of the book, "Your Kind of Beautiful", and ask students to make predictions about the story based on the title and cover illustrations.
2. Encourage students to share their predictions with a partner or in small groups.
3. Facilitate a brief whole-class discussion to gather students' predictions and generate excitement for the upcoming reading.

Explore (10 minutes):
1. Distribute copies of the book "Your Kind of Beautiful" to each student or pair of students.
2. Ask students to independently read the book or take turns reading aloud with their partner.
3. Instruct students to pay attention to any parts of the story that resonate with them or relate to building self-esteem.
4. After reading, allow students a few minutes to reflect on the story and jot down any thoughts or questions on sticky notes.

Explain (10 minutes):
1. Engage students in a whole-class discussion by asking the following questions:
   - What did you think about the story?
   - Did any parts of the story relate to building self-esteem and self-worth?
   - How did the characters in the story demonstrate social-emotional learning strategies?
2. Create a chart on the board or chart paper to record students' responses, highlighting key social-emotional learning strategies such as positive self-talk, empathy, resilience, gratitude, and mindfulness.
3. Provide explanations and examples of each strategy, emphasizing their importance in developing and enhancing self-esteem.

4. Encourage students to share their thoughts and experiences related to these strategies.

Elaborate (15 minutes):

1. Divide students into small groups and provide each group with index cards and writing materials.
2. Assign each group one of the social-emotional learning strategies discussed (positive self-talk, empathy, resilience, gratitude, or mindfulness).
3. Instruct the groups to brainstorm and write down practical ways to apply their assigned strategy

Dear Guardian,

You have an abundance of patience, you show it every day. Every day you wake up and give the warmest hugs, best advice and loads of unconditional love to humans who were not given to you biologically, without asking anything in return. Even though you did not endure or witness the pain associated with birth, you have experienced other challenges and difficulties.

For those sufferings you will be graciously rewarded, the children you are pouring into will blossom into incredible citizens. Continue to look ahead and trust that your unwavering commitment to your children is the right decision.

With love,
T & T

Developing Self-Esteem and Self-Worth

Topic:
Students will demonstrate the ability to apply a range of social-emotional learning strategies to develop and enhance their personal self-esteem and self-worth through the utilization of the children's book, "Your Own Kind of Beautiful"

Objectives:
At the end of this lesson, grade 11-12 students will be able to:

1. Identify and define self-esteem and self-worth.
2. Apply social-emotional learning strategies to develop and enhance personal self-esteem and self-worth.
3. Analyze the themes and messages of the children's book, "Your Own Kind of Beautiful", in relation to self-esteem and self-worth.

Prior Knowledge:
Students should have prior knowledge and understanding of:

- Basic concepts of self-esteem and self-worth.
- Social-emotional learning strategies.
- How literature can convey messages and themes.

Cue Set 1:
1. Begin the lesson by asking students to define and discuss the terms self-esteem, and self-worth in small groups.
2. Share the definitions and explanations with the whole class, highlighting key points.
3. Facilitate a brief class discussion on the importance of developing and enhancing self-esteem and self-worth.

Cue Set 2:
1. Introduce the children's book, "Your Own Kind of Beautiful" to the students.

2. Read an excerpt or summarize the book's content, emphasizing its themes related to self-esteem and self-worth.
3. Ask students to reflect individually on any personal connections they can make to the themes presented in the book.

Cue Set 3:
1. Share three social-emotional learning strategies (e.g., positive self-talk, setting achievable goals, practicing self-care) with the students.
2. Discuss each strategy, providing examples of how they can be applied to develop and enhance self-esteem and self-worth.
3. Engage students in a brief brainstorming activity, where they generate additional social-emotional learning strategies related to self-esteem and self-worth.

Direct Instruction Strategies:
1. Explain the importance of applying social-emotional learning strategies to develop and enhance self-esteem and self-worth.
2. Model the use of positive self-talk by sharing personal examples and inviting students to practice it together.
3. Guide students in setting achievable goals related to enhancing their self-esteem and self-worth, providing support and feedback as needed.

Practice Assignments:

1. Assign students to create a personal journal entry reflecting on their experience with positive self-talk and goal setting. Encourage them to express their thoughts, feelings, and any changes they observe in their self-esteem and self-worth.

2. Ask students to select one social-emotional learning strategy discussed in class and apply it in their daily lives for a week. They should document their experiences and outcomes in a reflection paper.

3. Provide a list of self-care activities (e.g., exercise, mindfulness, hobbies) and ask students to choose one activity to engage in regularly for self-esteem and self-worth enhancement. Students should write a reflection on how the chosen activity impacts them.

Team-Based Activities:

1. Divide students into small groups and assign each group a specific chapter or section from the book, "Your Own Kind of Beautiful."

2. In their groups, students should analyze the chosen chapter or section, identifying key messages and themes related to self-esteem and self-worth.

3. Each group presents their findings to the class, fostering a discussion on the different perspectives and insights gained from the book.

Formative Assessment Measures:

1. During class discussions and activities, actively observe students' participation and engagement, noting their understanding and application of social-emotional learning strategies.

2. Review and provide feedback on students' journal entries, reflection papers, and self-care activity reflections.

3. Assess the group presentations based on their analysis of the book themes and messages, ensuring they align with the concepts of self-esteem and self-worth.

Deep Questions:

1. How does positive self-talk contribute to the development of self-esteem and self-worth?
2. In what ways can social-emotional learning strategies support individuals in overcoming challenges related to self-esteem and self-worth?
3. How do the themes and messages conveyed in Your Own Kind of Beautiful resonate with your personal experiences regarding self-esteem and self-worth?

Remember to adapt the lesson seed according to your students' needs, pacing, and available resources.

Discussion Questions: "Your Own Kind of Beautiful"

After reading Your Own Kind of Beautiful, invite students to reflect on Daisy's journey and their own experiences. Begin by reading the provided questions aloud, then encourage students to think deeply before answering.

1. Daisy seems to have a perfect life, but she is unhappy with her hair. Why do you think she is unhappy with her hair?
2. What do you think about Daisy's hair? Do you like it? Why or why not?
3. What do you think about your own hair? Why do you feel that way?
4. What does the word diversity mean?
5. Why does the world need diversity?
6. Name something diverse about you.
7. Do you have a best friend?
8. What are some benefits of having a best friend?
9. What are some fun activities for best friends to do together?
10. What did Vivian say Grace and Daisy both share?
11. What is something that people with good hearts do?
12. What does it mean to be fearfully & wonderfully made?

Once the teacher or facilitator has asked the questions, move into a student-led discussion:

Objective:
To help students think critically, build empathy, and develop leadership in conversations about self-esteem, diversity, and friendship.

Instructions:
1. After the group answers the original 12 questions, explain:

"Now it's your turn to be the discussion leader. Think of a question you can ask the group that connects to Daisy's story, your own life, or what it means to be your own kind of beautiful."

2. Give each student 1–2 minutes to write a question in their manual (leave a lined space for this in the book).

Examples:
- "What's something you used to feel shy about but now love about yourself?"
- "How can we help a friend who feels unhappy about how they look?"
- "What's one way you can celebrate diversity at school?"

3. Students take turns reading their question aloud and allowing others to respond.

Remind students to listen respectfully and encourage one another.

"Your Own Kind of Beautiful" Diversity & Self-Love Circle

Objective
To help children explore their feelings about themselves, understand diversity, appreciate differences in others, and connect those ideas to kindness, friendship, and self-worth.

Materials:
Copies of the discussion questions (printed in the manual or on handouts)
Chart paper or a whiteboard
Markers
Crayons, colored pencils, stickers
Optional: Small handheld mirrors

Guided Story Connection (5–7 minutes)
1. Read or recap the key moments from "Your Own Kind of Beautiful", focusing on Daisy's feelings about her hair, her friendships, and her journey to self-acceptance.
2. Briefly explain the meaning of diversity in kid-friendly language: "Diversity means we are all different in special ways, and those differences make the world more beautiful."

Group Discussion (15 minutes)
Use the 12 discussion questions as conversation starters, but make them interactive:
For questions 1–3 (about Daisy's hair and their own hair):

Pass around a mirror. Each student says something they like about their hair before answering.

For question 4 (diversity):
On chart paper, write "Diversity" in the middle. Kids call out examples (skin color, talents, languages, hobbies, hair textures, family traditions).

For questions 7–9 (best friends):

Have kids pair up with their best friend (or a buddy in the room) and share a favorite activity.

For question 12 (fearfully & wonderfully made):

Invite them to share something that makes them feel "one-of-a-kind."

Creative Reflection: "My Own Kind of Beautiful" Page (15 minutes)

Give each student a themed worksheet with:
- A box labeled: "One thing that makes me unique is…"
- A second box labeled: "I am fearfully & wonderfully made because…"

Encourage them to use colors, patterns, and symbols that represent them.

Sharing & Affirming (5–10 minutes)
- Students who want to share can hold up their page and read their unique trait aloud.
- After each share, the group responds: "That's your own kind of beautiful!"

Reflection Questions
1. How can our differences make the world more interesting?
2. Why is it important to be kind to people who are different from us?
3. How can you celebrate your own kind of beautiful every day?

Draw the one thing that makes you unique.

```
┌─────────────────────────────────────────┐
│                                         │
│                                         │
│                                         │
│                                         │
│                                         │
│                                         │
└─────────────────────────────────────────┘
```

"I am fearfully & wonderfully made because..."

_____

_____

_____

_____

_____

_____

_____

_____

_____

Reflection Questions
How can our differences make the world more interesting?
Why is it important to be kind to people who are different from us?
How can you celebrate your own kind of beautiful every day?

_____

_____

_____

_____

_____

_____

_____

_____

_____

_____

_____

_____

_____

Discussion Questions: "Happy Being Me"

After reading "Happy Being Me", invite students to reflect on Daisy's journey and their own experiences. Begin by reading the provided questions aloud, then encourage students to think deeply before answering.

1. Daisy's favorite shoes were cowboy boots. What is your favorite pair of shoes, and what makes them special?
2. Daisy was teased for wearing cowboy boots. Is this a form of bullying? Why or why not?
3. Because of the teasing, Daisy was upset and needed someone to talk to. Who do you go to when you are upset? Why is that person your go-to?
4. If you were Daisy's friend or older sister, what would you say to make her feel better at that moment?
5. Have you ever been teased about your clothing/shoes/hair? How did you respond?
6. Daisy was taught to think positive thoughts when she is feeling sad. What do you do to cheer yourself up when you are sad?
7. If you see someone getting bullied or teased because of their clothes, what would you say to them? What would you say to the bully?
8. What is unique and special about you?
9. Would you be friends with someone who doesn't look like you/is different from you? Why or why not?
10. Why do you think people bully or tease other people?
11. What do you think the author means when she says, "Don't let people put you in a box"?
12. Explain what Creativity/Uniqueness/Individuality means.

Walk in My Shoes – Empathy & Individuality Circle

Objective

To help students explore empathy, understand how teasing affects others, and celebrate the unique qualities that make each person special.

Materials

The 12 Happy Being Me discussion questions (printed in the manual or on a board)
"My Shoes, My Story" worksheet (to be included in manual)
Colored pencils, crayons, or markers

Optional: Paper cutouts of cowboy boots, sneakers, sandals, etc., for decoration

Instructions

Guided Discussion (10–15 minutes)

Read the Happy Being Me questions aloud and allow students to share their answers.
For Question 1 (favorite shoes), write a few student responses on the board to show variety.
For Question 2 (bullying), have students raise their hands if they think it is bullying, and discuss why.

"My Shoes, My Story" Worksheet (15 minutes)

Provide each student with a worksheet that has:
An outline of a pair of shoes
A writing space labeled: "My shoes are special because…"
A second space labeled: "If someone teased me about them, I would remember…"
A final space labeled: "One thing that makes me unique is…"

Instructions to students:

Draw your favorite pair of shoes inside the outline — make them colorful and detailed.
Write a short paragraph or 3–4 sentences in the boxes provided.
Decorate the page with patterns or symbols that reflect your personality.

Empathy Circle Sharing (10 minutes)

Arrange students in a circle.

Each student shares their favorite shoes and why they're special.

Then, they read their "One thing that makes me unique" statement aloud.

After each share, the group responds with: "That's what makes you, YOU!"

Reflection Prompt

"One way I can support someone who's being teased is…" (lined space provided)

Extension Ideas

Kindness Pledge: Have students write one way they will stand up for others, and display the pledges in the classroom.

Optional Decorated Shoe Wall: Display all shoe drawings together to celebrate diversity and individuality.

Reflection

"One way I can support someone who's being teased is…"

Dear **GRAND**parent,

You have made a GRAND statement by stepping up to be a parent for the second time. Even though it may not have happened under the best circumstances, you are still equipped for such a time as this. You have experience, because you have made some errors along the way. Your experience and knowledge is invaluable as you navigate this familiar journey.

We believe that you already possess what it takes to give your grandchild the best shot at success. You may need a little support along the way, and that's okay. Trust yourself and remember that you did this a few years back and you can do it again.

With love,
T & T

Soft Skills

Soft Skills:
Personal attributes that enable someone to interact effectively with other people. Sometimes referred to as interpersonal skills, non-cognitive skills, or essential skills.

Examples include:
Communication
Organization
Problem-solving
Critical thinking
Conflict resolution
Time management
Leadership
Creativity
Teamwork
Adaptability

Soft Skills Activities

Activity 1: Telephone

Telephone is an age old activity designed to foster effective communication. The organizer begins the activity by lining the participants in a single file line. They may sit or stand. The organizer then whispers a predetermined phrase in the ear of the first person in line. They can create a short or long phrase, depending on the age of the participants.

NOTE: Once the phrase is whispered, it cannot be repeated.

The participant must then whisper the phrase in the ear of the next person until the phrase makes it's way down the line to the last person, who must then relay to the group what he or she heard in their ear. The organizer must then tell them what the original phrase was.

After completing the activity, engage the group in a discussion on the importance of paying attention to what others are telling you and to always make sure the words you repeat are accurate.

Example phrase: The blue dog took a walk in a red bandana.

Activity 2: Feelings Charades

For this activity you will need to write 10 emotions on individual index cards.
This can be prepared beforehand.
You will need a timer set for 15 seconds.

To begin, pair the participants into groups of two or you can choose to do this activity as a class. If you are pairing the participants, one will be the guesser, and the other will be the actor. If you are doing this activity as a class, there will be one actor, and a group of guessers.

To begin the activity, the actor will pull a card from the stack and act out the emotion written on the card using facial expressions and/or body language, only.
NO WORDS CAN BE USED.
The guessers will try to guess what emotion the actor is displaying. Each participant should be encouraged to participate as an actor.

Afterwards, the group will discuss what clues helped them guess the correct emotion.

This activity will:
- Foster discussions on identifying emotions
- Strengthen non-verbal communication skills
- Show how others may communicate their emotions in a different manner
- Encourage empathy for others
- Foster positive interactions with others

Activity 3: Puzzle Partners

For this activity, you will need age appropriate puzzles.

Encourage participants to work together to solve the puzzle. To make it more challenging, give the participants a time frame to complete the activity.

For an extra challenge , you can blindfold one member, who will act as the builder. The other member/members of the team are directors. Each director will give the builder a piece of the puzzle and "direct" them on where to lay the puzzle piece. The directors can use directional clues like higher, lower, left, right, down to the right, etc. The builders and directors can exchange roles after a pre-determined time.

Puzzles are a great resource for team building and communication. They force participants to collaborate, communicate, organize, and problem solve.

Mindfulness

Mindfulness teaches children and adults to be aware of what is happening right now, rather than dwelling on past events or what might happen later. It teachers how to pay attention to thoughts and feelings and respond intentionally rather than impulsively.

Mindfulness Activities

Activity 1: Deep Breathing

Inhale deeply for 4 counts, hold for 4 counts, and exhale for 4 counts. Repeat several times.

Activity 2: Mindful Walk

Take a walk outside and notice the sights, sounds, and smells around you. Encourage children to share what they observed on their walks and how these things made them feel.

Activity 3: Sensory Walk

Participants should note on their walk:

- 5 things they SEE
- 4 things they HEAR
- 3 things they TOUCHED
- 2 things they SMELL
- 1 thing they can TASTE

Activity 4: Gratitude Journal:

Write down three things you're thankful for and explain why.

Activity 5: Mindful Coloring:

Spend time coloring a mandala or nature scene, focusing on the colors and patterns.

After practicing these activities, children and adults should become more aware of our thoughts and feelings. When we are mindful, we become more resilient, and self- reliant, and often experience improved relationships because we are better equipped to regulate those BIG emotions that make us feel out of control.

Reflection & Growth

What activities did you enjoy most in this workbook?
How did practicing mindfulness make you feel?
Write about a time when you felt proud of yourself.
What goals do you want to set for the next month?

Reflection Questions
Write down three things you're thankful for and explain why.

_____

_____

_____

_____

_____

_____

_____

_____

_____

_____

_____

_____

Closing Words

As you finish this book, remember that every page, every activity, and every reflection was meant to remind you of one simple truth: you are valuable, unique, and worthy, just as you are.

The skills you've practiced here, kindness, confidence, empathy, creativity, and mindfulness—are tools you can carry with you every day. They will help you face challenges, build strong friendships, and celebrate the beauty of diversity in the world around you.

Whenever you need a reminder of your own strength, open these pages again. Revisit your drawings, your affirmations, and your words. They are proof of your growth and your own kind of beautiful.

Keep shining. Keep believing in yourself. And never forget—there is only one you, and the world is better because you're in it.

Answers begin with a purple letter with the rest of the word in blue.

a	c	c	o	u	n	t	a	b	i	l	i	t	y	r
s	c	o	m	m	u	n	i	i	a	t	i	o	n	e
e	s	s	c	i	t	i	z	e	n	s	h	i	p	s
l	e	e	g	o	t	r	e	s	t	c	z	o	g	p
f	l	l	r	h	m	i	r	e	s	p	e	c	t	o
r	f	f	a	u	a	p	r	n	y	e	e	n	a	n
e	e	w	t	k	c	m	a	w	g	r	a	c	e	s
s	s	o	i	i	o	u	l	s	t	i	o	n	e	i
p	t	r	t	a	u	l	o	w	s	n	g	a	e	b
e	e	t	u	p	r	s	s	i	o	i	p	a	c	i
c	e	h	d	r	a	r	i	t	e	r	o	b	i	l
t	m	n	e	s	g	y	a	d	a	p	t	n	o	i
s	p	s	h	j	e	c	o	n	f	i	d	e	n	t
h	o	n	e	s	t	y	i	e	m	p	a	t	h	y
t	l	m	k	a	k	i	n	d	n	e	s	s	e	q

Citizenship   Empathy   Kindness   Accountability

Compassion   Grace   Self esteem   Communication

Responsibility   Gratitude   Self respect   Respect

Confident   Honesty   Self worth   Adapt

www.ingramcontent.com/pod-product-compliance
Lightning Source LLC
Chambersburg PA
CBHW061113070526
44583CB00027B/3284